CUSTERIANA MONOGRAPH SERIES

Custer Observed:
General Custer
Through The Eyes Of
Monroe Evening News'
Karl Zeisler

Custer Observed: General Custer Through The Eyes Of Monroe Evening News' Karl Zeisler

Preface by
Stephen T. Gray

Introduction by
Dean C. Baker

Monroe County Library System
Monroe, Michigan

ALL RIGHT RESERVED TO REPRODUCE OR TRANSLATE

THIS WORK IN ANY FORM OR BY ANY MEDIA

Copyright © 1988
by the
Monroe County Library System
and
Monroe Evening News

ISBN 0-940696-14-2

*Printed by the
Monroe County Library System
Graphic Services Department
Monroe, Michigan*

Contents

Preface i

Introduction iii

June 25, 1938 1

May 6, 1939 7

April 13, 1940 13

June 28, 1941 21

August 28, 1948 31

September 18, 1948 37

January 29, 1949 43

June 23, 1951 49

July 26, 1952 55

January 3, 1953 61

The Monroe Evening News

Karl Zeisler at work at the Monroe Evening News, June, 1950.

Preface

Karl F. Zeisler, author of these 10 columns dealing with the history and lore of General George Armstrong Custer, wore many hats. He was a journalist, an author, an educator and – throughout his other careers – a historian.

The columns reprinted here represent only a tiny portion of his historical work centering on the heritage of Monroe, Michigan. They originally were published in The Monroe Evening News in his column entitled, "The Observer."

Mr. Zeisler was born in Lancaster, Ohio, in 1903 and spent part of his childhood in Monroe. After graduation from the University of Michigan in 1926, he worked as a reporter for a wire service and two other newspapers before returning to Monroe as managing editor of The Evening News in 1930.

His column, "The Observer," made its debut in 1937. It appeared regularly in The Evening News for 20 years, chronicling the long history of this early French settlement on the shore of Lake Erie. The stories of General Custer reprinted here only touch on the rich historical legacy he left for residents of Monroe.

Mr. Zeisler continued writing his column for The Evening News even after leaving the paper in 1946. He became a visiting professor at UM in 1947 and a full-time faculty member in 1952, teaching journalism for another 20 years before retiring in 1972. He died in the fall of that year at the age of 69.

Surely nothing would make Karl happier than knowing that his loving research lives on in this volume.

Stephen T. Gray
Editor
Monroe Evening News

Introduction

Reading these columns from The Monroe Evening News by my late friend and colleague at the University of Michigan, Professor Karl F. Zeisler, not only renewed my respect and admiration for the man, but gave me a new perspective on his subject, General George Armstrong Custer.

Many books and articles have been published about Custer – many highly critical of him; in contrast to earlier works which depicted Custer as a hero, contemporary writers have tended to assess the disaster at the Little Big Horn as a massacre of Custer's own making. Professor Zeisler has done what a good journalist should do: he has researched and assembled the facts and contemporary accounts, and has left it to his readers to judge whether General Custer was solely responsible for his own death and the deaths of his men. This reader is strongly persuaded by these columns that he was not.

These columns are not critical of the Indians, either; indeed, Professor Zeisler has told their side of the story with fairness and no little sympathy. Of other white men of the time in the West and of some of Custer's fellow officers, he is more critical. This is not surprising to anyone who knew him, and especially to his colleagues in the press and in journalism education, for while he was one who held strong opinions on many issues, he was always fair and restrained in presenting and discussing these views. It was written of him in a profile of him in The Michigan Alumnus some years before his sudden death of a heart attack at his home in Ann Arbor in 1972 that he was "a journalist's journalist." Karl and many of his associates on various newspapers might have preferred "a newspaperman's newspaperman," but either would surely apply.

This is not to say that Karl was a roughneck type from "The Front Page." He graduated from the University of Michigan with honors in English and a Phi Beta Kappa key, and he was later admitted to that select group, Mensa, made up of persons with an IQ of 130 or more. His professional life was not all in newspaper journalism and journalism education, either; he wrote for and was a recognized authority on magazines and magazine article writing, and prolific free-lance writer of articles for a wide variety of publications, a keen student of history (as these columns attest), a public-spirited citizen as his membership on a number of committees and commissions demonstrates, and a teacher whom students, too, admired and respected.

"Drawing from a background of long professional experience," said The Michigan Alumnus in its article, "his classroom delivery is polished and articulate. Students also appreciate his informal ease, warm personality, and the patent genuineness of his interest in the progress of their studies."

Karl began his career in journalism at age 14 when he worked for local newspapers in Monroe and then Ypsilanti as both a carrier boy and a mechanical apprentice. He was born in 1903 in Lancaster, Ohio, spent his early years in Monroe and his high school years in Ypsilanti, where he first attended Eastern Michigan University. Later, he enrolled at the University of Michigan, where he was a correspondent for the Detroit Saturday Night, Chicago Herald-Examiner, New York Herald Tribune and Christian Science Monitor. On the Ann Arbor campus, he was associate editor of Michigan Chimes and an honors student in English. His future interest in General Custer may have been sparked by his first jobs after graduation, for he traveled west, ending up in Denver as an employee of the International News Service, as State House, City Hall, courthouse and police reporter. After a year, he moved on to San Jose, California, as telegraph and city desk assistant and real estate editor for the Mercury Herald. From there, he returned to Michigan in 1928 as editorial writer and assistant telegraph editor of the Pontiac Daily Press. Returning to Monroe in 1930, he became managing editor and editorial writer for the Evening News, which he served in these capacities until 1946, when he assumed the duties of associate editor, editorial writer and special writer.

A family man after 1927, when he married the former Alma A. Wardroper in Ypsilanti, Professor Zeisler was the proud father of a son, James F., born in 1930, and a daughter, Katherine, born in 1932; he and his wife also eventually doted over five grandchildren.

Their families and wide circle of friends always found warm hospitality at the Zeislers' spacious home on a large corner lot in Ann Arbor Hills, with their Christmas Eve gatherings and their annual corn roast picnic in the fall especially notable events. The corn was grown in their extensive vegetable garden on their property, and Karl personally presided over the grills on which it was roasted. Friends from Monroe and from elsewhere in Michigan, as well as his Journalism Department colleagues and their wives, made it a point never to miss these affairs, and usually everyone stayed until a late hour, singing around the grand piano in the Zeislers' living room. Among those attending would be the publishers of two weekly papers at whose shops Karl and a group of journalism students each summer took over all the writing, editing, and makeup work in a "living lab" of incalculable value to the aspiring journalists. Karl's circle of friends in Monroe ranged from a printship owner to a former prosecutor and state legislator, and most of them came to Ann Arbor each fall for the picnic.

At the time of his untimely death, Karl Zeisler had accumulated an impressive record of published work and of professional and community service. He had been a visiting lecturer at the University from 1947 to 1951, when he became a full-time associate professor (and later professor). In addition to his campus courses, he taught correspondence courses in creative writing through the University's Extension Department that received national recognition, and he was frequently invited to instruct and address writers' conferences. He was also frequently invited to speak on Northwest Territory history, the mass media and career opportunities in them, and on free-lance writing.

Karl's nonfiction work appeared in American Mercury, Atlantic Monthly, Antioch Review, Collier's, Editor and Publisher, Journalism Quarterly, Quill, Nieman Reports, Federal Probation Quarterly, Library Journal, Rotarian, and the National Observer. As a researcher, he did studies on readability and communication in graphic arts, propaganda and public opinion, taxation and assessment, community organization, and history of the Northwest Territory, Great Lakes, Michigan, and Monroe County. For the Michigan Historical Commission, he wrote "Your Community Writes Its History," for the Monroe

Public Schools, "A Child's History of Monroe," and for the Bureau of Business Research of the Graduate School of Business Administration, Ann Arbor, "Industrial Use of Water in Michigan."

Karl was also a member of the State Historical Society of Michigan, Monroe County Historical Society, Washtenaw County Historical Society, Ann Arbor Citizens Council, Association for Education in Journalism, American Association of University Professors, Sigma Delta Chi, and in 1950 he was delegate from Michigan to the Midcentury White House Conference on Children and Youth. He was vice chairman of the Michigan Youth Commission and served as chairman of the Governor's Teen Age Driver Safety Committee. He also served on several state committees for Michigan Week.

It may therefore be said that his output of a column a week for 20 years for the Monroe Evening News, of which these ten columns on Custer are a small part, represents a significant portion of his writings during a most productive life.

> Dean C. Baker
> Emeritus Professor
> Department of Communication
> University of Michigan

June 25, 1938

- *June 25, 1876*
- *Prophet Without Honor*
- *Is Monroe Ashamed?*
- *Colonel Bates's Story*

SIXTY-TWO years ago today, under the burning mid-afternoon sun of the Montana plains, General George Armstrong Custer met his death at the hands of 2,500 Sioux and Cheyenne Indians, who surrounded his command of 193 enlisted men and annihilated them in a massacre that to this day arouses heated controversy. Today Custer's name is recalled in a thousand places scattered around the world, yet in Monroe, his boyhood home, the scene of his marriage and the town he loved most to return to on furlough, no official recognition is given to the sixty-second anniversary of the Battle of the Little Big Horn.

For even in Monroe the Custer controversy persists. In all frankness it must be said that he is more honored elsewhere than in the town that can more rightfully claim a reflected share of his glory than any other. True, Monroe persuaded the state some years ago to erect a monument to the man who was a brevet brigadier general at 23, a brevet major general at 24 and a hero of the Civil War whose exploits in that conflict brought him to the attention of President Lincoln and were only overshadowed by the catastrophic termination of a brilliant military career. But for all his close association with it, Monroe has no written records of Custer, no collection of even the local mementoes he left, no repository of the vast number of relics that would make his life vivid to youngsters and the city a Mecca for students of Custer.

The writer of the most recent popular biography of Custer did not even bother to extend his researches to Monroe, which he refers to as a "town on the shore of Lake Michigan." Even at Cadiz, near the hamlet of New Rumley, Ohio, where Custer was born, a considerable collection of Custer lore exists. Elizabeth Bacon Custer, offended by Monroe's removal of the general's monument from the courthouse square to the park, left all her collection to West Point, none to her home.

• • •

Here The Observer must interpose a personal bit to emphasize the point. After a boyhood spent in Monroe, during which like other youngsters he had flung snowballs at the bronze military figure on horseback, he began to travel through the West. Wherever he went on the prairies he found evidences of Custer's greatness, of the honor and respect in which he was held by westerners. Soon he began to be ashamed of himself for having to acknowledge that he had lived in Monroe and knew so little of Monroe's great soldier. He learned far more about Custer in the West than he has since been able to piece together in Monroe.

In another column today is an account of a Custer collection in a German museum. Last week newspapers headlined a tragic train wreck in Custer Creek named for the general in Montana, and not far from the scene of his last battle. In the Black Hills of South Dakota is the town of Custer, where the general camped in 1874 on that ill-starred "scientific" expedition to confirm the presence of gold in the Indian's sacred dwelling place of the Great Spirit, and where, in another Custer Creek, one of the general's soldiers panned gold, starting the great "days of '76" gold rush. A Custer elm is still preserved in Kansas, near Fort Hayes, on a piece of ground once owned by Custer, and "bounded on the north by Canada and on the south by Mexico and the Rio Grande," according to his description.

The Army cherishes the memory of Long Yellow Hair, the Indian fighter. The general and his wife repose in peace at West Point, where an impetuous youth first learned military discipline, and left with the last class graduated on the outbreak of the Civil War to fight for the Union. The Army chose his name for its greatest wartime cantonnement in Michigan. But since June 4, 1910, Monroe has done nothing to perpetuate the memory of her great soldier, whose Seventh Cavalry recruited many of its members from this community.

• • •

Did Monroe, back in 1876, feel too keenly the shame of that bloody massacre on the shores of the Little Big Horn? Did it side with the detractors of Custer, who blamed his impetuosity, his dare deviltry, his vanity and his egotism for the defeat? Has the memory of that bitter news from the West lived on here to make the town ashamed of its adopted son? Or was Custer disliked by the community that scorned a swashbuckling, uniform-flaunting, long-haired Ohioan who dashed along its streets on a fiery military mount, and transmitted that instinctive distrust from generation to generation? The Observer must confess he cannot understand Monroe's attitude toward George Armstrong Custer, its indifference to the opportunities to share in his fame, its disregard of the potentialities in a name that is magic wherever it is spoken outside his onetime home.

There is at least one Monroe native who does not share this local feeling toward Custer. He is Colonel Charles Francis Bates, now of Bronxville, New York, who lately visited Monroe to pursue his devoted studies of the general's career. Colonel Bates, who was born on a farm across the Raisin from the Custer homestead, is assembling material, much of it entirely new, for the writing of a definitive biography of Custer, one which he hopes will be truly popular in the sense that it will be readily available to a large number of readers. On this sixty-second anniversary of the Custer Massacre, The Observer takes pleasure in reprinting Colonel Bates's account of what happened along the Little Big Horn on June 25, 1876. In a privately printed account of "Custer's Indian Battles," published on the sixtieth anniversary of Custer's death, Colonel Bates tells the story graphically.

Custer had set out in May of '76 on the long-awaited campaign against the Sioux, who had left the Indian agencies and were in revolt against the white man. He had divided his command with Captain Benteen in charge of a scouting force and Major Reno heading a flank movement. Custer followed the high bluffs along the Little Big Horn to attack the gathering of Sioux and their Cheyenne allies and sent Reno down the valley. Reno had met an unexpected outpost of Indians, engaged in a brief encounter, and seeing the Indian squaws rushing to shelter, believed the entire encampment was charging his force. He retreated into the woods, and panic-stricken, gave the order to retreat. Meanwhile Custer, thinking that Reno would carry out the flank movement, pushed ahead on the bluff. When he encountered a force of Cheyenne and a moment later was attacked by the Sioux who had sent Reno's men scattering, he sent word back to Benteen for reinforcements, ordered the reserve ammunition brought up and began a strategic retreat that would expose the pursuing Indians to attack by both Benteen and Reno.

• • •

Here Colonel Bates takes up the story:

But Reno and Benteen did not come. Terry and Gibbon were more than a day's march away, and Custer and his men had to meet alone the overwhelming numbers of the Indians. In previous Indian fights, when white soldiers had called for help, every available man had been hurled to their relief no matter what the odds.

There is no doubt that Custer's men, with dogged courage, fought long and well. Their resistance must have lasted at least two hours. The issue of the battle was more than once in doubt, according to all the Indian accounts. The squaws, who had returned to the village after Reno's retreat, began to take down the tepees, preparing for flight. At this period of the battle Chief Two Moons said he could not break the Gray Horse Troop – the company near Custer. Sitting Bull, the great medicine chief of the Sioux, who took no part in the fight, said when he recounted the story he had heard from his braves, "They (the soldiers) kept in pretty good order. Some great chief must have commanded all the time."

In a tumult of shouting and in blinding clouds of dust, Custer and his men fought till their last cartridge was gone. A terrible sense of loneliness swept over them. For a soldier to die bravely is one thing; to die calmly and with perfect discipline when he knows himself abandoned is quite another. Custer's men fell company by company as they stood, though the rough features of the ground made their lines for the most part irregular, and they had taken advantage of every elevation which offered protection.

At last their guns had all been silenced and Indian battle axes had completed their horrid task on the wounded. Most of the bodies were scalped and mutilated, but Custer they did not scalp because they recognized that he was a great chief and had fallen bravely. He lay surrounded by his men, his two brothers (Captain Tom and Boston Custer) and a nephew (Autie Reed) near him and his brother-in-law (Lieutenant Calhoun, who married Maggie Custer) not far away. It was thus the soldiers found him when Terry and his men came two days later. One of his officers who knew him well said, "He had crossed his feet and lay as if asleep, taking one of his catnaps as we had so often seen him do on the short halts on the march."

Though he met his death at the hands of the Sioux on the Little Big Horn River, near Hardin,

Montana, and between the Black Hills and Yellowstone Park, Custer was really the victim of the white man's treachery in dealing with the Indians. The Sioux and other plains tribes were enraged by the successive invasion of their territory, climaxed by the gold rush into the Black Hills, by wholesale cheating on the part of politically appointed Indian agents and by the continued violation of treaties they held sacred. Custer, sent to check their revolt, was made the victim of their bitter and desperate revenge. The Battle of the Little Big Horn was the greatest loss suffered by the white men in their conflict with the plains Indians and hence caused an undying controversy, to which fuel was added by the dissension in the Seventh Cavalry between Custer and Reno and Benteen.

May 6, 1939

- *Pointed Memories*
- *Backyard Romance*
- *News from Bighorn*
- *The Widow's Return*

FRANKNESS is an exceedingly rare quality, and all the more charming when it is found, all too seldom, in personal reminiscences. The sonorous platitudes and banalities in which most history, personal and community, comes down to us from the past is one of the principal reasons why most of us regard history as a dull subject; when the historian really says what he thinks and is utterly frank in his opinions we prick up our ears and reading becomes a delight. Such unpretentious and unguarded history, with which we may not all agree but will certainly find readable, comes from the lips of Mrs. C. W. Hockett, and was found by W. C. Sterling, president of the historical society, in the May leaflet of the Burton Historical Collection, published in Detroit.

Mrs. Hockett, who was the daughter of Mayor Herman J. Redfield, recorded her memories of Monroe in an interview July 11, 1938, in Detroit, where she lives at 17610 Parkside avenue. She is now nearing her eightieth birthday, having been born in Monroe in June, 1859. Her father was Monroe's nineteenth Mayor, serving from 1871 to 1874, when his daughter was in her teens.

"Mother and father had three children who died in infancy before I was born," she recalls. "Father was very fond of me and used to take me with him on many occasions. I lived at Monroe until I was 23 years old. I have kept up my Monroe connections ever since." Here, then, is Mrs. Hockett's remembrance of Monroe in the seventies:

● ● ●

You ask me, "Have I any theory as to why so many men

from Monroe went into the army?" No, I did not know that this was true. Of course, there was a whole regiment of the Navarres; there was Colonel Bates; the Smiths, Colonel and General Smith, two different families, no relation; and many other army officers of higher rank, but I hadn't thought of trying to explain why they chose the army rather than the navy. Monroe, of course, was a sort of cradle of great men for Detroit – Governor Alpheus Felch, Robert McClelland and many others.

(It is interesting in this connection to note Judge Christiancy's reason, given in last week's Observer, why so many leaders of Michigan chose Monroe as their home. He believed it was Monroe's location at the head of Lake Erie and the assumption on the part of intelligent men in the 1840's that railroads would never be important rivals of water transportation, hence Monroe would thrive as the chief port on the most important water thoroughfare to the West – Lake Erie. That they were mistaken was the irony of fate, but may account for the conservatism that dominated the city for so many years – Observer's note.)

Monroe was the center for the education of young ladies, too. The Young Ladies' Seminary was famous in its day. Mrs. John Bagley was among the first class that graduated from the seminary. I attended there in the later years. The school's equipment was considered good for its day. Professor E. J. Boyd was the head. The seminary was later sold to the first St. Francis Home and conducted as a school for a few years. St. Francis Home later was built next to the Ford Highland Park plant, and still later, receiving a large sum of money for the Highland Park property from Henry Ford, built their present home.

What do I know about the Joys and Mortons? Edward Morton was editor of the old Monroe Monitor. Frank Morton was an uncle of Joy Morton. There was an Emma Morton. Then there was a relative, a Bijah Joy. Bijah was an old-time policeman of Detroit and figured in the M. Quad newspaper articles. (M. Quad was the pen name of a Free Press editor.) Joy was a brother of Mrs. J. Sterling Morton, the mother of Joy Morton. The Mortons were a large family; Mark, Carl, who died here, Paul and others.

The Bacon family? Well, Elizabeth Bacon was the daughter of Judge Daniel S. Bacon. Her mother died and she had a stepmother. Libby married General Custer, but Mrs. Custer was just "Libby" to everyone in the town. The Custers were Methodists. They came up from Ohio. General Custer was born in Ohio. One of his older half-sisters married David Reed and came on to Monroe. Young Custer went to her home and from there attended school in Monroe. His father was a blacksmith. He later got a pension. I think. The name originally was Koester – German. The general probably inherited his bravery from his mother's side.

We did not associate with the Custers. They were quite ordinary people, no intellectual interests, very little schooling. Father and Mother Custer came to Monroe to live after the son became famous and had married Libby Bacon. Mrs. Welt, who is now living at the Belcrest Hotel was Tillie Meyerfeld. The Meyerfelds and Custers and Bacons lived near each other. Young Custer got a little job working for the Bacons. He used to hang around the backyard and wait for Libby. He was not received in her home.

He was of good character but the family just couldn't see him. After he became famous for his military service, however, the judge finally consented to their marriage. They had a large wedding. Custer was wise – he came home on furlough and was married in his uniform. Margaret Custer, his only sister, was a fine girl. She became quite a cultured lady. She attended Miss Noble's school here in Detroit. She had a little circle of friends in Monroe that she entirely ignored later in life. Frequently when she came to

Detroit we would go to the old Opera House together. She married Lieutenant James Calhoun. She was one of the girls the general took out West. After Calhoun was killed she married a man by the name of Maugh who was from the East.

I must tell you about the day we first learned of the tragic deaths of the men in Custer's brigade. I remember so well, it was on the Fourth of July (1876). I was sitting upstairs by the window mending. I was 17 years old, and I saw father coming up the street, his coat off, his vest off, his hat in hand, and waving a paper, the old Detroit Tribune. It was about 11 o'clock in the morning.

He came in and called "Minnie! Minnie!" Minnie was not my name but father often called me by it. I flew downstairs for I knew something awful had happened. There he stood, white and chalky, with the paper shaking in his hands.

"General Custer's entire brigade has been wiped out!" he gasped. "Think of it, Autie, Lieutenant Calhoun, Ross, Tom, they're all gone!"

It was perhaps a week after the tragedy happened that the news reached us. It came through by a boat passing down the Missouri River with the crew shouting. "The whole Custer brigade has been wiped out!" The news then came through to the Detroit papers. It was during the height of the Hayes and Tilden Presidential campaign.

A great silence came over Monroe, then all the bells began to toll – church bells, firehouse bells, every bell in town. To this day I never hear a bell toll that it does not bring back the memory of that dreadful day. A telegram was sent immediately to Emma Reed. She replied, "It's true!" The whole town was crushed. They mourned, "Our General Invincible is dead!" The bells continued to toll all day. Public meetings were held in the courthouse.

General Custer's nephew, George Armstrong Reed, was

among those killed. We used to call him Autie. Autie was the life of the party. He went to all the dances and we thought a great deal of him. It had been his ambition to join his uncle and at last the time had come when he was 17 and he was permitted to go. I remember him so well (Mrs. Hockett was about a year younger than Custer's namesake – Observer's note.) I used to like to go over to his house. (The Reed house was on the northeast corner of Monroe and Fourth, now the Firestone station.) They had a room literally filled with Indian costumes and things that his uncle had sent them. I used to love to dress up in these war bonnets. They had a rack of guns and spears, and a hat rack which was about 20 feet long and made from an elk's head. The general had brought the head from the plains. Almost the last time I saw Autie was when a girl friend and I went to a fire (it was a custom in those days to run to fires) and he was there.

It was some weeks before the widows came home. Dave Reed went right out and got his son's remains and brought them back. When the women came back the whole town turned out. Professor Boyd took mattresses and laid them over slats in wagons and went down to the station and got Libby and Maggie. Poor Maggie was in such a state they thought she would lose her mind. Judge Bacon had died by this time but Father and Mother Custer were alive and Libby went there.

Mrs. Custer remained in Monroe about two years, then she was offered a position in New York with the Decorative Arts Society. She had received most of her art training in the seminary at Monroe. Later she earned some revenue from her books. Her business affairs in Monroe were left in the hands of John Rauch, an attorney, but something went wrong and he lost all of her father's holdings. After that, as long as John Rauch lived, she did not come back to Monroe. She would come as far as Toledo and Charles Wing would go there and confer with her. I was an art student in New York about that time and she was my chaperone. Maggie Calhoun married again later in life. Some other widows went East.

• • •

To older residents of Monroe, Mrs. Rockett's recollections are an old story, but to younger residents they may help reconstruct some of the flavor and background of a community in which dwelt an aristocracy as proud and as able as any in the new West.

April 13, 1940

- *$1,000 for a Slave*
- *Port Difficulties*
- *Curly's Story*
- *Tom Custer's Heart*

SEVERAL weeks ago the indentured servant, a virtual slave who agreed to work without pay for several years to secure passage from England to America, was mentioned in this column. Looking over some recent acquisitions at the historical museum in the Sawyer building the other day The Observer came across a deed transferring ownership in a slave. The deed, not the slave, came into the possession of W. C. Sterling's grandfather, and has been added to the museum collection. The legal process by which the state of Louisiana permitted a slave to be sold might be worth repeating:

Before me, William C. Smith, recorder... personally came and appeared Eliza Ann Blankenship, the wife of George Rossiter, herein authorized and assisted by her said husband, has this day bargained, sold, transferred and delivered and do by these presents grant, bargain, sell and deliver unto Valen I. Bird of the the same residence a certain Negro girl named "Delilah," aged about 16 years, of dark complexion and slave for life, to have and to hold unto the said Valen I. Bird, his heirs and assigns forever, the said Eliza Ann Rossiter warranting said slave to be free from all the vices and maladies prescribed by law. She further warrants the title of said slave against herself, her heirs and assigns and all others legally claiming the same, unto the said Bird, his heirs and assigns forever. The above sale is made for and in consideration of the sum of one thousand dollars in hand paid, the receipt whereof is hereby acknowledged.

The instrument is dated December 14, 1857, three years before the outbreak of the Civil War, one war that was fought in a good cause. Incidentally, Mrs.

Rossiter, who sold her slave Delilah for $1,000 cash, seems to have had difficulty in signing her name. It is outlined in pencil and traced waveringly in ink.

• • •

Dr. Alfred I. Sawyer, builder of the home housing the museum, was Mayor of Monroe in 1877. Among his papers presented to the museum by Miss Sawyer is a resolution passed by the common council on January 17, 1871, which shows plainly how Monroe had to struggle year after year for the maintenance of its port, visited this week by the first ship of the navigation season and prepared, after many more years of struggle, to receive vessels and cargo of all kinds. Extracts from the council's resolution:

Whereas, for a series of years, through appropriations by the general government and money raised by local taxation, we have used every effort to improve the harbor of our city and make this a commercial point for the ready shipment of the large amount of produce from the interior of our state, which seeks an outlet elsewhere, but would naturally and more cheaply come here for transportation and a market if our navigation was good – the capacity of our harbor being yet far short of what is now necessary for the ingress and egress of boats and vessels of the largest class, and far short of the wants and demands of a large area of country which will soon be dependent upon this point for an outlet as a result of the early extension of the Flint & Pere Marquette Railway, now under contract for construction to Monroe, with its 273 miles of track and its northwestern connections beyond our state, and

Whereas, the navigation of the Canal and River Raisin is yet so imperfect that it is with great difficulty, delay and extraordinary exertion and injury to property as the last season has shown, that our business men engaged in forwarding are able to load, discharge and navigate vessels of even light draft – which is in part done by lighters, and

Whereas, the recommendations of distinguished members of the corps of topographical engineers, as early as 1828 and subsequently show Monroe to be a point for the favorable consideration of the general government, the report of Colonel Kearny, who was especially appointed by the Department to classify the harbors of the lake in 1838, placed Monroe in the first class, and designated it as "one of the few which constitutes the first class," which fact has been verified by all the captains upon the lake . . . therefore be it

Resolved, . . . that the Honorable F. C. Beaman, our Representative in Congress from this district, be earnestly requested to present and advocate a bill in Congress . . . providing for an appropriation of sixty thousand dollars to finish the work on the River Raisin and the Canals, constructed by the United States Government . . . so as to render it navigable for vessels of the first class and make it a safe harbor of refuge therefor.

To find out whether Congressman Beaman got the $60,000 would require a long and tedious search through War Department files, proceedings of the council or elsewhere; fortunately, however, the answer to this and many more questions about local history will eventually be provided by the work of a group of six young people assigned to the task by the NYA. Howard Johns, county NYA supervisor, two weeks ago started the project of indexing all the bound volumes of local newspapers, under the joint sponsorship of the Monroe County Library System and the Monroe County Historical Society. The young people are working now on copies of the Monroe Commercial of 1853 in The News office, making minute notes on every item of local interest recorded in this invaluable storehouse of community information. When their work is completed it will be assembled into a card index making accessible names, dates and references to local happenings over a period extending back for a century. No more important historical task has ever been undertaken in Monroe County.

• • •

From many women of present-day Monroe The Observer received kind assistance in filling out the names of Monroe women who had figured in the community's commercial and cultural life, in response to a recent column mentioning a few of these women. Mrs. Jennie S. Wallace wrote that she was "greatly surprised that nobody happened to mention the name of Mrs. Crump and her children's school on East Second street. The house stood about where Martin Weickert's house does now. Miss Ada Crump taught in the grades (they called them grammar grades to the present eighth grade)." Miss Gertrude Golden recalled that Miss Reilly, who kept the hat shop on the upper bridge at Monroe street, was named Mary instead of Nancy. And Miss Carrie Boyd said Miss Uhl's shop was on Washington street, not on Monroe street.

Evidence of the abiding interest in Custer (at least outside of Monroe) comes from T. G. Finzel, who writes from Kenmore, New York, enclosing a clipping from the Buffalo Evening News of March 22. "Custer Massacre Blamed on Lack of Good Scouting," reads the headline, and a picture shows Frederick H. Turner, Buffalo resident and former government scout on the plains. Mr. Turner, now 87, rode 190 miles to the Little Bighorn five days after the massacre and talked with Curly, Custer's Indian scout, one of the "only" survivors. Here is Scout Turner's version of the battle:

Buffalo Bill would have known how many Indians there were and Custer wouldn't have started the fight (if a scout as skilled as Buffalo Bill had been working for Custer.) Curly knew there was going to be a massacre right when the fight started. He fell off his horse and pretended to be dead. Then he got under an Indian blanket and crawled away. The last he saw of the two Custers (George and Tom) they were slashing away with their swords. Custer might have had a chance, Curly said, but the Indians had 16-shot Winchesters while Custer had only single-shot breechloading rifles. The soldiers' rifles got so hot they couldn't get their shells out. The ground was torn up for half a mile around as if a hurricane had struck. It was a sad sight. There were dead horses, broken guns and swords strewn all over.

After the massacre the squaws tomahawked and knifed them all except General Custer. Sitting Bull said Custer was so brave he wasn't scalped. True to the prediction of Chief Rain-in-the-Face, Tom Custer was found with his heart cut out. The Indian chief said he would cut Tom's heart out and eat it . . .

Well, old scouts all have their own versions. It is always interesting to hear both sides. Several years ago when George F. Hoffman was attending the International Livestock Show in Chicago he struck up a conversation with the man in the next seat.

He happened to be J. E. Erickson of Montana. Learning that Mr. Hoffman came from Monroe, Mr. Erickson gave him a copy of the Teepee Book, official publication of the fiftieth anniversary of the Custer Battle, published at Sheridan, Wyoming, in the semi-centennial year, 1926. Full of Custer lore, the book contains the following statement written by Scout Curly, an Indian:

What I am going to tell is just short. I don't know much about it, but I will tell you all I know. I was never where most of the soldiers were; I was always with Custer's outfit. I knew the Chief with the long whiskers and I knew Custer's brother. I also knew the one who called the bugle. We met the camp before 10 o'clock in the morning. Just before we got to the camp there was one band went one way and the other band (Reno's command) went the other way. I don't know anything about the other band because they were away across the river.

On my side I have told you all I know. The bugler got killed in the camp. Some of them got killed in the river. They (the Sioux) would not let the soldiers cross the river. There were too many of the Sioux. The soldiers got down to the ground by the river but could not get across so turned and ran back up the hill. The soldiers did not know much about fighting. These white people know more about fighting than the soldiers did. All the soldiers were killed before 10 o'clock.

Just before they got all the soldiers killed, and there were just a few of them left, my horse was a pretty good runner and he ran off. I was just a young fellow and Custer told me to run off and I did run off. I was only 16 or 17 and didn't know much about fighting at the time. If I had been older when they had the war I might have done something and if I had been older I wouldn't have run off; I would have stayed there and got killed. I had to run away. They did not chase me. I went east to the Agency, where the big pines are, and stayed there. After I got off the high hill I rode to where the steamboat was. I brought the letter over to where they had the fight; brought it from the big chief back where they had the war.

That's Curly's story as he remembered it in 1926. As for the story that Rain-in-the-Face cut out Tom Custer's heart, the Teepee Book has the chief's own account of the battle, told on his death bed to a noted Indian scholar, Dr. Charles A. Eastman. Here are extracts:

While I was eating my meat we heard the war-cry. We all rushed out, and saw a warrior riding at top speed from the lower camp, giving the warning as he came. Then we heard the reports of the soldiers' guns, which sounded differently from the guns fired by our people in battle. I ran to my teepee and seized my gun, a bow and quiver full of arrows. I already had my stone war club, for you know we usually carry those by way of ornament. Just as I was about to set out to meet Reno, a body of soldiers appeared nearly opposite us, at the edge of a long line of cliffs across the river.

All of us who were mounted and ready immediately started down the stream towards the ford. There were Ogallalas, Minneconjous, Cheyennes, and some Unkapapas, and those around me seemed to be nearly all young men.

"Behold there is among us a young woman!" I shouted. "Let no young man hide behind her garment!" I knew that would make those young men brave. The woman was Tashenamani, or Moving Robe, whose brother had just been killed in the fight with Three Stars. Holding her brother's war staff over her head, and leaning forward upon her charger, she looked as pretty as a bird. Always when there is a woman in the charge, it causes the warriors to vie with one another in displaying their valor.

The foremost warriors had almost surrounded the white men, and more were continually crossing the stream. The soldiers had dismounted, and were firing into the camp from the top of the cliff. Then the soldiers had mounted and started back, but when the onset came they dismounted again and separated into several divisions, facing different ways. They fired as fast as they could load their guns, while we used chiefly arrows and war clubs. There seemed to be two distinct movements among the Indians. One body moved continually in a circle, while the other rode directly into and through the troops. Presently some of the soldiers remounted and fled along the right ridge toward Reno's position, but they were followed by our warriors, like hundreds of blackbirds after a hawk. A large body remained together at the upper end of the ravine, and fought bravely until they were cut to pieces. I had always thought that white men were cowards, but I had great respect for them after this day.

It is generally said that a young man with a war staff broke through the column and knocked down the leader (Custer) very early in the fight. We supposed him to be the leader because he stood in full view swinging his big knife over his head, and talking aloud. Someone afterward shot the chief and he was probably killed also; for if not, he would have told of the deed, and called others to witness it. So it is that no one knows who killed Long-Haired Chief (Custer).

After the first rush was over coups were counted as usual on the bodies of the slain. You know four coups or blows can be counted on the body of an enemy, and whoever counts the first one is entitled to the first feather.

Many lies have been told of me. Some say that I killed the chief, and others say that I cut the heart out of his brother, Tom Custer, because he had caused me to be imprisoned. Why, in that fight the excitement was so great that we scarcely recognized our nearest friends! Everything was done like lightning. After the battle we young men were chasing horses all over the prairie, while the old men and the women plundered the bodies; and if any mutilating was done, it was by the old men.

The canard about Chief Rain-in-the-Face cutting out Tom Custer's heart has often been disproven, but like many other legends of that famous battle, it crops up time and again. As long as there remain survivors of that era in which the battle was fought, there will be different versions of what happened.

June 28, 1941

- *Desecration For Gold*
- *Black Hills Lark*
- *Invading El Dorado*
- *Sitting Bull's Revenge*

GOLD was the direct cause of the terrible vengeance wrought by Sitting Bull and the Sioux allies on General George Armstrong Custer, his two brothers, Tom and Boston, his nephew Autie Reed and the 261 members of five troops of the Seventh Cavalry on the Little Big Horn just 65 years ago on June 25. What we know as the Custer Massacre was in reality the Sioux's revenge for Custer's "desecration" of the Black Hills of South Dakota two years before. Custer had invaded the sacred refuge of the plains Indians, which the Sioux had wrested from the Crows only a generation or two before, and Custer had to pay the penalty. Except for this invasion of the Black Hills, Custer had the respect as well as the wholesome fear of the plains tribes. But for despoiling the abode of the Sioux gods, and causing an irresistible tide of prospectors, Custer would never have met with the horrible fate that beset him and his command on June 25, 1876, on the slope above the Little Big Horn River in Montana. The story of Sitting Bull's revenge on Monroe's famous Yellow Hair really begins with the now forgotten expedition into the Black Hills.

The "hills" are really mountains – the highest and most extensive range in the country east of the Rockies themselves. They are now traversed yearly by a host of tourists who little realize,

---

The ubiquitous Observer wrote today's column last Thursday, June 25th, the 65th anniversary of the battle he describes. He wrote it in the Black Hills of South Dakota only a few miles from where Custer's expedition passed on its way out of the hills. – The Editor.

---

save for the many roadside markers designating the hanging of horsethieves or the massacre of early prospectors and settlers by Indians, the tremendous hardships encountered by the pioneers who followed Custer into the hills in search of the elusive yellow dust. In the 65 years since the hills were opened over 440 million dollars worth of gold and 65 million dollars worth of silver have been taken from their rugged mountains and gravelly streams. That gold was present in the hills had long persisted as a rumor, but historians of the hills today are convinced that the Indians never found gold there themselves. They merely referred to gold in their possession as coming from the dark and mysterious region of the Black Hills, which they feared themselves to enter because it was the home of spirits.

But the rumors persisted. In the spring of 1874 General Phil Sheridan returned from a trip to the plains and secured War Department permission to send an exploring expedition into the hills to determine if they had any mineral resources and if they were suitable for settlement. He ordered General Alfred H. Terry, in command of the western forces, to put General Custer in command. This was 25 years after the gold discovery in California, and the interest manifest in the possibility of another such El Dorado is evident from the size and expense of Custer's expedition. It was formed at Fort Abraham Lincoln, across the Missouri River from the boom town of Bismarck, North Dakota, the terminus then of the Northern Pacific. It included 1,000 men, the Seventh Cavalry and two companies of infantry, 100 Indian scouts, 110 wagons each drawn by six mules, 1,000 cavalry horses, 300 beeves for provisions, 3 gatling guns, a military band, an engineer, geologist, naturalist, botanist, photographer, several newspaper correspondents, and two practical placer miners, Horatio N. Ross and William T. McKay. It was the largest and most elaborate exploring expedition ever fitted out in the West. And for Custer, fretting at the inaction of his new command at Fort Lincoln, it was a lark, pure and simple. He reveled in it, and and enjoyed every minute of it, as his glowing reports of the beauties of the hills, the abundant game, the colorful wild flowers, the mineral wealth and the agricultural possibilities amply testified.

• • •

The party, four long columns of canvas-covered wagons, flanked by columns of cavalry and trailed by the infantry batallion, with Custer and his staff including the scientists at its head, moved out of Fort Lincoln with the band playing July 2, 1874, for a sixty-day trip that was to take them across 883 miles of virtually unexplored country, part of which Custer and his troops were to retrace just two years later in the Yellowstone Campaign which led to the Little Big Horn. They entered the hills from the northwest, instead of from the logical northeast because their guides insisted the wagons could not be taken through the hills, But Custer, after exploring a cave in which a white man's skull and many Indian relics were found, and climbing 6,000-foot Inyan Kara peak west of the hills (although the view of the range itself was obscured by the smoke of prairie fires set by the Sioux to spoil the grazing) insisted on turning into the hills themselves. After the heat, the alkali dust and the swarms of grasshoppers on the prairie, the cool, shady glades in the hills, with their sparkling spring water and rich grass, their inspiring views, their awesome red, green and purple coloring, their fields of flowers, their open meadows or "parks" and their heavy pine and spruce woods seemed indeed like the paradise Custer described them.

Maps show the route of the lengthy caravan and markers in the hills today show much of the route, which The Observer recently retraced. How the heavy wagons ever traversed the steep, narrow, rocky gulches, cut through the dense pines, forded the swift streams and found passes through the rugged foothills, without accurate maps or competent guides (none of the Indians with the party had every penetrated the hills) is today inconceivable. Roads following the route are a marvel of engineering. But nothing could stop Custer. Every day he spurred on ahead of the plodding wagon train. He quizzed the few frightened Indians encountered on the trails. He hunted daily; over 1,000 deer as well as two grizzlies (one killed by Custer himself), antelope and elk were shot in the hills. Every high ridge castellated rock and lofty peak Custer had to climb himself. He named the crags and gulches. He explored the wildest canyons, and his descriptions of some are accurate even today. An objective of the party for several days was Harney Peak, marked on the crude maps as the highest point in the hills (it is 7,200 feet high, the loftiest peak west of the Rockies) and named for General Harney, who had passed near the hills on his Indian campaigns. Finally they circled the peak to the south and made camp in the French Creek Valley. This was immediately called Custer Park by the members of the expedition, though Custer himself referred to it as Golden Valley, for obvious reasons. Today it is at the edge of Custer State Park, largest state park in the country. Here the first camp was made on the site of what is now the city of Custer, and from here General Custer, with a cavalry troop and a group of scientists, made the first ascent of Harney, blazing the trail which still winds up its rugged southern slope. Custer was disappointed in not being able to scale the topmost crag, as the party did not reach the summit until sundown, but he wrote his name and that of his companions on a piece of paper, inserted it in an empty cartridge and stuck it in a cleft in the rock. The explorers got back to camp at midnight.

Hills historians are in dispute as to exactly when and where the most significant event of the expedition occurred. It was in Golden Valley, or Custer Park, apparently in that first camp on the present site of Custer. And it probably occurred on July 30, a month after the expedition left Fort Lincoln and the day before Custer's ascent of Harney. At any rate, Ross and McKay, the prospectors, had been vigorously panning gravel from every creek the party crossed, but on French Creek they first produced tangible evidence that there was gold in the hills. Ross is believed to have panned out the first dust. That night in Custer's tent, he unwrapped a piece of paper and laid out about 50 tiny grains of gold on the commander's desk. Custer described them as averaging the size of a pinhead – others said they could only be seen under a reading glass – the total value of a day's panning couldn't have amounted to over a few dollars, but it was gold. The camp there and then experienced the first attack of gold fever, the white man's disease that proved fatal two years later on the Little Big Horn.

• • •

Next day every man in the camp, from major to mule skinner, in the words of William E. Curtis, correspondent of the Chicago Inter-Ocean, crowded "around the diggings, with every conceivable accoutrement, shovels and spades, picks, axes, tent pins, pot hooks, bowie knives, mess pans, kettles, plates, platters, tin cups, and everything within reach that could either lift dirt or hold it, and put into service by the worshippers of that god gold, and those were few who did not get a showing, a few yellow particles clinging to a globule of mercury that rolled indifferently in and out of the sand."

Gold was really what Custer had come into the hills elaborately equipped to discover, and although the geologist was very disparaging of the placer diggings, Custer lost little time in getting word of Ross's discovery off to civilization. Nearly a week was spent in the French Creek vicinity while exploring parties were sent out in all directions. Then Custer ordered camp broken and moved southwest through the hills to a point on the prairie. There at midnight on August 3, Charley Reynolds, a white scout who was among the many of Custer's command who became separated from the troops on the Little Big Horn and was shot down after his ammunition was exhausted in a lone stand against the Sioux, set out for the nearest telegraph station at Fort Laramie, Wyoming, to break the news to the waiting world. For the Custer expedition had been widely publicized, and everyone knew why it was defying Sitting Bull and the hostile Sioux to enter the sacred Black Hills. Reynolds, according to one hills legend, wrapped his horse's feet in gunny sacks, and according to another, had the regimental blacksmith put the horseshoes on backward to throw the Indians off his trail.

Miraculously he got through the Indians, who were up in arms about the military invasion of their territory, and on August 27 the Chicago Inter-Ocean scored a monumental beat with Curtis's graphic account of the discovery of gold in the Black Hills. Here is its historic headline:

GOLD

The Land of Promise – Stirring News from the Black Hills

The Glittering Treasure Found at Last – A Belt of Gold Territory Thirty Miles Wide

The Precious Dust Found in the Grass under the Horses' Feet – Excitement Among the Troops

And so on – the account ran down two columns on page 1 and continued three and a half columns inside, along with an editorial saying: "It would be a sin against the country and the world to permit this region, so rich in treasure, to remain unimproved and unoccupied," and urging "speedy measures" by the government to open it to the whites. For the hills were a part of the Sioux territory, excluded from settlement, and any white man who ventured into them did so at his own risk. The treaty of 1866 had pledged the government to keep settlers out of the territory.

Today there is an imposing monument to Prospector Horatio N. Ross in a park in the little town of Custer, and a log cabin is filled with relics of the early prospectors. What happened when the Inter-Ocean's thrilly tale circulated throughout the country is another story – of the hundreds who ventured into the hills in search of gold, of their encounters with the Indians, of the government's effort to round them up and send them home to make a show at least of respecting the treaty, of the rapid development of the hills despite these efforts, of how Custer grew from the site of the expedition's two-day camp to a city of 11,000 in less than two years and of the subsequent wealth and tragedy bound up in gold – of Wild Bill Hickock and Calamity Jane, of Deadwood Dick and Flyspeck Billy who was the first man hanged in Custer, of the treasure stage from Deadwood to Cheyenne, of all the wild and unbelievable characters and crimes of the Days of '76.

But to get back to Custer and his expedition. After dispatching Reynolds with the fateful news of the gold discovery on August 5, Custer led his party north through the hills and out on the prairie past Bear Butte, retracing the 300 miles across the plains to Fort Abraham Lincoln, where they arrived on the afternoon of August 30. Here Custer busied himself with a formal report on the expedition to supplement the three hasty reports he had dispatched by scouts en route, mailing it from Bismarck on September 8. In it he noted the presence of gold in the hills, as well as iron, gypsum and plumbago, but cautioned against any attempt to dig out these minerals until more extensive surveys had been made and the Indian title had been extinguished. He recommended that the government open the hills to settlement, emphasizing their rich agricultural possibilities. He pointed out that the Indians themselves not only did not occupy the hills, adopting toward them a "dog-in-the-manger attitude," but actually used them as a route for the illicit traffic in arms and as a refuge for the bad Indians who got off the reservation to make sorties against white settlers.

Meanwhile, in that same month of September, 1874, two men, Collins and Russell, were recruiting the first gold expedition into the hills at Sioux City, Iowa, secretly, because General Sheridan had heard of their plans and ordered frontier army posts to turn back any gold seekers bound for the hills. But on October 6, the Collins-Russell party, consisting of 26 men, a woman and her 9-year-old son, crossed the Missouri and headed for the new El Dorado. They spent a miserable winter in a stockade on French Creek near Custer's camp, a stockade which has now been reproduced for the benefit of tourists, and were herded out in the spring by the troops, with only a handful of gold to show for their winter's placer mining. That was the start of the invasion of the hills, however. By 1876 the mother lode, in the quartz strata on Deadwood Gulch, had been discovered, Deadwood and Lead replaced Custer as the boom towns of the hills, and the army found its task of policing the hills rendered impossible by the very numbers of the gold seekers.

● ● ●

Meanwhile Sitting Bull, the medicine man and leader of the Sioux, was brooding and making plans for revenge. It was only natural that the Sioux should have resented the Custer expedition, but they were of course far more concerned by the influx of prospectors it brought to their sacred hills. For this they held Yellow Hair to blame, and to avenge the violation of the abode of the gods they gathered, in the spring of 1876, under Sitting Bull, on the prairies of Montana. There they could send out war parties to murder white settlers, and there they could quickly find refuge in the Big Horn Mountains if the soldiers attacked in numbers. General Crook made a futile attempt that spring to drive them from the banks of Rosebud Creek; subsequently the Yellowstone Campaign was ordered by General Sheridan, and Generals

Terry and Custer, the former in command, set out to join Crook and rout the gathering tribes.

What happened on the Little Bighorn was thus the direct sequel to the Black Hills expedition of 1874. Custer's lark, the fun and adventure of penetrating the region which the Indians had always pointed to as the land of mystery and strange terrors, turned in two brief years to Custer's Last Stand. The gold, from which neither Custer nor any member of his command was ever to profit, brought the hordes of white men into the Black Hills, and Sitting Bull won bloody revenge for the desecration of the abode of the spirits.

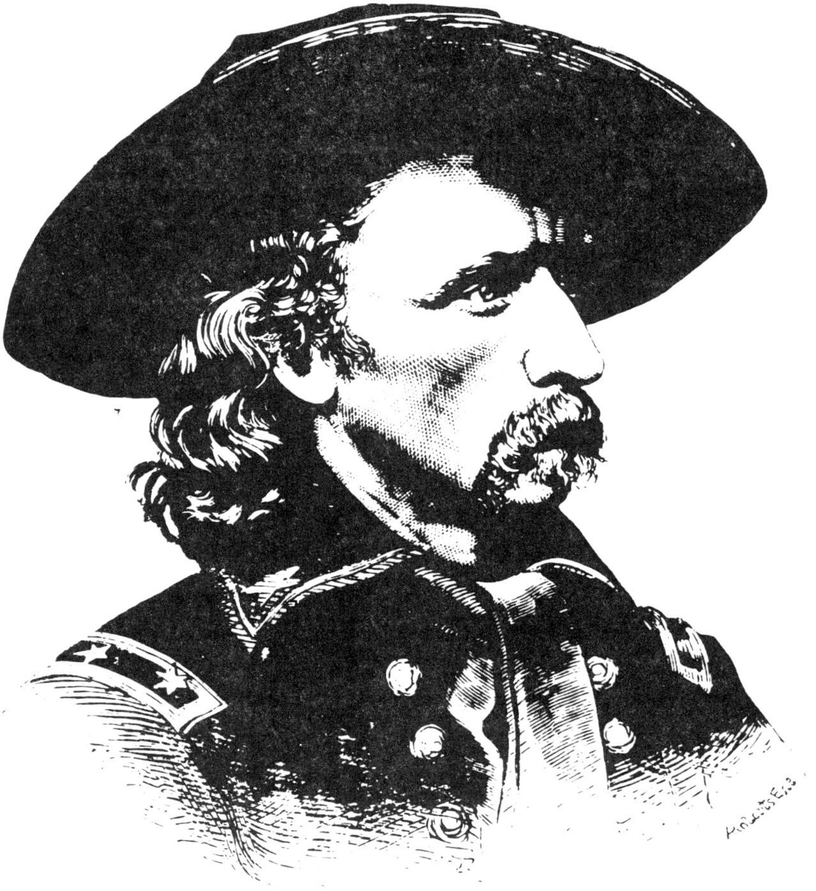

Truly Yours
G. A. Custer

August 28, 1948

- *Romance of Custer*
- *Letters to Libbie*
- *Love Finds a Way*
- *Reinstatement*

MONROE continues to receive attention in the current magazines. George Paxson, former president of the Monroe County Historical Society, called The Observer's attention to an article on Custer in the September "Esquire." Written by Wessel Smitter, it deals with a much publicized episode in the military life of George Armstrong and Elizabeth Bacon Custer, the very one, in fact, for which the general was court martialed and spent the subsequent summer in Monroe as a civilian. That was in 1868, after Custer had been placed in command of the Seventh Cavalry Regiment for action in the sporadic warfare against the plains Indians. "The General Fell in Love," as it recounts this episode in the current "Esquire," reads as follows:

"A few years ago, no self-respecting saloonkeeper would have been caught dead without a picture of Custer's Last Stand in the place of honor behind his bar. As far as most of us inveterate barflies know, General George Armstrong Custer spent his whole life fighting Indians. At any rate, we don't often think of him as a great lover, in spite of his golden curls and his liking for fancy, self-designed uniforms. He was immune to fatigue, hunger, thirst and the lack of sleep. He loved a hard ride and a tough march, and in feats of strength and endurance he was more than a match for any man in his regiment. Yet, though he was a hard master and ruled his troopers with a strong hand, his deep and gentle devotion to his young wife, Elizabeth, is something worth talking about.

"In Boots and Saddles, one of the books Elizabeth Custer wrote after her husband's death, she says that he prepared the water for her bath and warmed her clothes before the fire when she dressed in the morning. It was like that. Wherever he went, he took her with him – and he had to go to some pretty rough spots on the American frontier. Invariably, when campgrounds were muddy, he carried her from her mount into the crude wooden barracks which were to be their quarters. They sat side by side at the table when they ate together. He insisted, when writing his magazine assignments, that he was unable to work unless she was seated on the opposite side of his desk, and when she overstayed while calling on a neighbor, he sent her nightgown to her in the hands of the most stalwart soldier he could find. On one occasion Custer sent his orderly with a facetious note asking whether she would like to have her trunk sent over to the place where she was visiting.

• • •

"While on his scouting expeditions, Custer sent daily letters of prodigious length to his 'Dear Libbie.' She writes: 'For several slow, irksome months I did little else than wait for the mails, and count each day that passed again. I had very interesting letters from my husband, sometimes 30 or 40 pages in length.' In order to maintain a regular exchange of correspondence during their long separations, Custer dotted the plains with courier stations, each stocked with fresh mounts and swift riders, between himself and the home barracks where his wife waited in lone wretchedness. It was no small expense to the government.

"Whatever fame Custer may have gained comes largely, as I have said, from his dramatic exit from life on the Little Big Horn; but he had a loving, loyal biographer, who saw in him the finest, most heroic of men. Elizabeth Custer lived 57 years after the death of her hero. There were no children, and she devoted her long widowhood to preserving his memory with books and articles filled with praise and adoration of her dead husband. Other biographers, less afflicted by love's myopic influence, say that Custer was no military genius – that bad generalship got him into tough spots and that good luck brought him out, but that at the Little Big Horn his luck deserted him. That may be true, but Elizabeth Custer considered more things than military strategy and Army tactics. She weighed her hero in balances heavily weighted with a deep understanding, as well as a unique devotion.

"In one of her books she says: 'If I was put in charge of any one in the regiment, he asked them to kill me if the Indians should attack the camp or the escort on the march.' Custer's superiors regarded this as the negative approach to the problem of dealing with a young wife who was always seeking some new pretext for joining her husband in some distant camp, but it was all right with her, who counted the reward and not the cost, if the orders came from her husband. Both knew even better, perhaps, than Custer's high-ranking superiors, the kind of fate that awaited a young beautiful woman, once she had been captured and held by the Indians.

• • •

"Once General Sherman, Custer's superior, sent her this note: 'You had better remain quietly at Fort Riley as your husband will be on the march all summer.' 'Quietly!' she lamented. 'He may talk about living quietly, but I cannot.' It was during this same campaign that connubial love found a way, although a costly one, to bring the two together. On the pretext of returning to his base camp for supplies, Custer selected an escort of 75 picked riders and horses, and left his regiment leaderless on the plains. The ride that followed was seldom duplicated, even among great plainsmen.

"Custer and his small band of veteran troopers made a forced march of 150 miles to Fort Hays in 55 hours. At Fort Hays he left behind those of his escort who were too spent to go on, and rode 60 mile to Fort Harker, in 12 hours. There he left the remainder of his escort and went on, without rest, to Fort Riley, where Elizabeth Custer was waiting. It was a magnificent feat of endurance and a spectacular example of human stamina, but it was bad soldiering. Custer's superiors charged him with disregarding orders, with being derelict in his duties, with doing great damage to valuable government-owned horses, and with failing to recover the bodies of two men who fell behind during the ride and were killed by Indians. These matters Elizabeth Custer barely mentions in her reminiscences. But she describes the meeting with her husband.

" 'After days of such gloom,' she writes, 'my leaden heart quickened its beats at an unusual sound – the clank of a saber on our gallery and with it the quick, springing step of feet unlike the quiet infantry around us. The door . . . opened and, with a flood of sunshine that poured in, came a vision far brighter than even the brilliant Kansas sun. There before me, blithe and buoyant, stood my husband . . . There was in that Summer of 1867 one long, perfect day, It was mine, and blessed be the memory, and it is still mine, for time and eternity.'

• • •

"Custer was ordered to stand a court martial, and the counts were against him. His punishment was that he be removed from his command for one year and that he forfeit his pay for the entire period. It was a severe sentence, but they were together, and who shall say that the price was too great for a long summer day that was theirs 'for time and eternity?' On a tragic June day in 1876. Custer and all his heroic troopers lost their lives to the Sioux in the Battle of the Little Big Horn. He and Elizabeth had been married but 12 years. I for one like to forget about Custer's Last Stand. I prefer to remember that he made a forced march of 210 miles and risked a court martial just for a day with the woman he loved."

So much for "The General Fell in Love." The sequel is of equal interest to Monroe. Soon after the sentence began, Custer's old cavalry commander in the Civil War, General Phil Sheridan, was transferred to Fort Riley, where Custer and his wife, the former Libbie Bacon of Monroe, stayed on. General Sheridan immediately turned over his own quarters as commandant at the post to his court martialed lieutenant colonel. In the summer of 1868 the Custers came home to Monroe, and lived with Judge Bacon in the old homestead then on the site of the post office. All during that time the Indians were restless over the influx of new settlers on the plains, the depletion of their hunting grounds and constant friction with the Army. Sheridan immediately set about trying to get Custer, his favorite cavalry leader, reinstated. There was a sharp division in the Army at that time, with a pro-Sheridan and a pro-Grant faction. Grant had reviewed Custer's conviction and confirmed it.

But when General Sully took Custer's old command on a foray against marauding Indians and was driven back ignominiously to Fort Riley, Sheridan moved in earnest. Representing the rising Indian unrest as real warfare, he demanded that Grant send Custer back to the Seventh Cavalry because he was "young, very brave even to rashness, a good trait for a cavalry officer, and ready and willing now to fight the Indians." In September Sheridan dispatched the following telegram to Custer in Monroe: "Generals Sherman, Sully and myself and nearly all the officers of your regiment have asked for you and I hope the application will be successful. Can you come at once? Eleven companies of your regiment will move about the first of October against the hostile Indians, from Medicine Lodge Creek toward the Wichita Mountains."

• • •

Custer, leaving Libbie behind, left by train at once for Kansas. On the way his reinstatement caught up to him, and early in October he began whipping his regiment in shape for the campaign that was to reach its climax in the bloody battle of the Washita, in which Custer's troops wiped out a whole Indian village.

September 18, 1948

- *The Custer Legend*
- *Visit to Battlefield*
- *Sioux Reunion*
- *Five in One Family*

THIS summer Dr. L. A. Frost, president of the Monroe County Historical Society, took a busman's holiday and traveled extensively in the West, visiting museums and historical shrines in many states. To a Monroe resident such a trip is always illuminating because it reveals the extent to which Monroe's General George A. Custer is regarded as a hero – in fact, the leading hero – of the West and its settlement and development. Wherever Dr. Frost went he found museum visitors primarily interested in displays of Custer material, some of it pretty meager, to be sure, and every community with the slightest claim to a connection with Custer exploiting it to the fullest extent. Yet Monroe, with a far more substantial claim, and with far more material available, can be visited by thousands of tourists each summer who may never realize that this was his home unless they happen to drive by the monument.

Many a Monroe resident first comes to realize what a figure General Custer cuts elsewhere in the country by travel in the West. As a case in point, The Observer has received a letter from First Lieutenant Richard W. Curry, now stationed at Richland, Washington. Lieutenant Curry writes as follows:

"Being a subscriber to my home town paper and an ardent reader of The Observer I cannot pass without comment the previous articles in which General Custer has been discussed. In my trips to and from the west coast I have always made it a point to stop at the park and battlefield monument on the Little Big Horn River, and look out from the hill on which are placed the headstones where those brave men of the Seventh Cavalry fell. There you will find names that are common in and around Michigan. As I walked up this hill that is above the valley of the Little Big Horn River and approached the monument I could realize a bit of the thoughts of Custer as he waited in vain for help to come.

• • •

"The Indians of the Rosebud and Crow Agency in this vicinity still acclaim him as a great leader and fighter. Only when you have traveled over this land and seen the routes of his marches and battles can you realize his achievements. Even when he was greatly out-numbered he was at his best. And the fighters of all nations respect this. Having been more than curious as to the General's record, I have gone to the files that are at the convenience of Army personnel and have found that his record is very high. In parallel with all great fighters his was truly a great record of service and achievement. If he had been alive today he would rank with Generals Patton, Hodges, Terry Allen and Harmon, Americans, Air Marshals Tedder and Cunningham, English, and Marshal Smuts of South Africa.

"These men all had their so-called bad moments in warfare and as yet have never had the full respect of the noncombatant writers of history. Only by the men who followed them into battle are these men respected and loved. Again in appreciation of your column I say keep up your work as it is well that the people learn and remember these truly great Americans. We need all the Americans we can get."

The Custer legend, outside of Monroe, is still very much alive. The following Associated Press dispatches from Rapid City, South Dakota, tell their own story: "Ten Indian survivors of Custer's last stand which the Sioux call the Battle of the Little Big Horn are to get together again, Carl Burgess, Superintendent of the Custer State Park, said that a ceremonial powwow in the park likely will be the last of its kind. The Indians, all

Sioux, will come from the reservations in North Dakota, Nebraska, Wyoming and South Dakota. Oldest of the Indian survivors of the battle – which ended in the slaying of the 275 soldiers of the famed U.S. Seventh Cavalry under the leadership of General George Armstrong Custer – is Iron Hawk.

• • •

"The battle took place June 25, 1876, when Custer and his command invaded the Little Big Horn territory in search of 'hostile Indians.' The army had planned to trap the Sioux with three forces. Custer's forces, however, made contact with the Sioux before junction with the other units. Believing only 800 Indians were before him, Custer led his command deep into Sioux territory and was ambushed by more than 2,000 Sioux warriors."

And after the reunion: "Six of the Indians who took part in the Custer massacre held a reunion yesterday. They are old men now, but as to the massacre they call a battle, their opinions are unchanged. They'd do it again. The warriors, whose ages range from 78 to 98, still are proud of their people's triumph over the white general at the Little Big Horn. They are only sorry the Sioux are not strong enough to chase the white man out of their hunting grounds and their Black Hills, which they believe to be inhabited by the Great Spirit. The six celebrants who were at the Little Big Horn when General Custer and his command were annihilated are Iron Hawk, 98; Dewey Beard, 88; High Eagle, 87; Comes Again, 84; John Sitting Bull, son of the famous chief, 80; and Little Warrior, 78. At least two other Sioux who were at the massacre are living."

Commenting on the powwow, the "Detroit Free Press" said editorially: "Out at Rapid City, South Dakota, six Sioux Indians claiming to be the only survivors of that battle which wiped out General Custer and a squadron of the Seventh Cavalry are brushing up their war bonnets for a reunion powwow. The superintendent of Custer State Park thinks probably it will be their last one. They are old men now – the oldest, Iron Hawk, 98. We suppose there is some sermon here on the mollifying effect of time's passage. In the days when no well-regulated saloon was without its lithograph of Custer's last stand, there undoubtedly would have been a public howl of outrage at the idea of his enemies being permitted to hold a reunion to reminisce about the Sioux's great day on the Little Big Horn. Now the gathering is barely noted. But there is a still more significant footnote on time in the fact that, when World War II came, not one Sioux had to be drafted. The tribe was insulted at the idea that any Sioux would fail to volunteer. Old Phil Sheridan probably would like to have seen that. When he was an Indian-fighting general he once said that with 20,000 Sioux cavalrymen he could lick any army Europe could turn out."

• • •

Just to show that interest in the Custer story is long-sustained, H. F. Mathews recently brought to The Observer a clipping in the collection of Simon F. Navarre, taken from a Detroit paper printed in May, 1910. It shows pictures of five members of the Custer family slain in the massacre. "The accompanying picture shows the three Custer brothers, their brother-in-law and their nephew," reads the article, "all five of whom were killed in the Battle of the Little Big Horn against an overwhelming force of Sitting Bull's Sioux June 25, 1876. The photograph from which the General's picture was made was taken but a few months before his death, when he was in his 37th year, and is Mrs. Custer's favorite.

"The general's two brothers who met death in the battle were Lieutenant Tom W. Custer and Boston Custer. Tom was 31 at his death. During the Civil War he enlisted as a private in an Ohio volunteer regiment and rose to the rank of lieutenant colonel before he was 21. He was twice decorated with the medal of honor for on two occasions in battle personally seizing and capturing as trophies Confederate regimental flags. He entered the regular service as lieutenant in 1866 at the same time as his brother, who had been a major general of volunteers, was commissioned lieutenant colonel of the Seventh Cavalry. In 1874 Lieutenant Tom, by a ruse, enticed Rain-in-the-Face, an Uncpapa renegade, to an agency post in South Dakota and springing upon his back, held him until he was disarmed. Rain-in-the-Face had murdered two citizens for robbery. He was in a fair way of being hanged when he escaped from the guardhouse, and was next heard of swearing vengeance. He joined Sitting Bull's band, and is said personally to have shot both the General and Lieutenant Tom at the Little Big Horn.

"Boston Custer was 28 at his death. His home was in Monroe, and he had at no time seen army service. He had been of consumptive tendency and was advised that an open air existence on the plains would be beneficial to him. The General had him appointed forage master of the Seventh Cavalry; he was on that duty during the ill-fated expedition. In Monroe he was familiarly known as Bos. Lieutennant James Calhoun, whose wife was Maggie E. Custer, the sister of the Custer boys, married her at Monroe March 7, 1872. Lieutenant Calhoun entered the service as a private in a regular regiment during the Civil War. He was the General's adjutant in the Indian campaign.

• • •

"Autie Reed, son of the General's sister, Mrs. David Reed, was his favorite nephew. The General's full name was George Armstrong Custer, but even when a small boy he was always in the family called Armstrong, or Autie. Autie Reed was named for him. Autie was just finishing his course in the Monroe high school in the early summer of 1876 when the General was on a visit to Monroe. It was then known

41

through the newspapers that an Indian war was pending and that General Custer's command was to be in it. Autie wanted badly to see an Indian fight and his uncle yielded to his pleadings to take him. But as Autie could not go as a guest the General detailed him for duty along with another schoolmate to help drive the herd of cattle which were taken with the expedition to be slaughtered as fresh beef was needed.

"The bodies of Boston Custer and Autie Reed are buried at Monroe. General Custer's remains lie in the cemetery at West Point, his alma mater. The bodies of Lieutenant Tom Custer and Lieutenant Calhoun are interred in the military cemetery at Fort Leavenworth, Kansas."

Thus the Custer legend, then as now, excites the interest of people all over the country – except in Monroe. Some day Monroe will awake to the opportunities it has long neglected to capitalize on Custer's fame, and make proper provision for the display of the Custer material available here. When that day comes Monroe will be amazed at the abiding interest in the life and career of the man whose spectacular leadership and love of battle made the West safe for settlement.

January 29, 1949

- *Custer Monument*
- *Fr. Crowley's Part*
- *Local Organization*
- *Success at Last*

MENTION was made last week of a benefit concert given for the Custer Memorial Association back in 1907, and it was noted that the association had been revived from a previous effort to establish a monument to the cavalry hero here after his death in the Battle of the Little Big Horn in 1876. Nothing came of that earlier effort, though for a year after the battle local papers were full of the enterprise. The original association was handicapped by the fact that the General's body was taken to West Point for burial and national attention focused on a suitable monument to him there, rather than in Monroe, his home. Energetic local citizens took up the torch in Monroe again, however, after the local success in getting the state to appropriate funds for the Kentucky Soldiers' Memorial on South Monroe Street. Their efforts were eventually rewarded, as recorded in this account taken from a local paper dated June 21, 1907:

"Monroe gets $25,000 for a Custer monument. It was sudden news – unexpected, no longer hoped for – after all, very good news. For the moment, factory sites and new industries are forgotten and every man, woman and child in Monroe is talking Custer monument. How did it happen? Who did it? Who would have thought of it? Such questions caught one's ears at every turn when on Wednesday morning the news began to circulate that the bill had passed both houses of the legislature.

"It had gone through the senate Tuesday evening, but was supposed to have been effectually smothered in the lower house. All the political surgeons pronounced it dead and its friends were preparing to gather about it in its final pigeon hole and prepared to say: 'Don't it look natural?' And even the attorney general shook his head sadly and said: 'The fellow that resurrects that bill is a dandy.' But they did not know, or else had forgotten, that down in these parts there resides the Rev. Fr. Michael J. Crowley; also that aside from running his church (St. John's) and congregation very successfully, he has many and influential political friends at Lansing and knows as well as any politican how to make use of that friendship in a good cause; also that he is the match of almost any of the politicians, when he can fight on the side of right and conscience; also that it was through his efforts, influence and tireless work that the bill ever passed the senate.

• • •

"Well, on Tuesday evening Fr. Crowley received the news that it had passed the upper house, but had met with fatal treatment in the house of representatives. He knew the conditions and had practically no hope of winning out, but determined to make one more try. He used his telephone, called up every person of influence in Lansing, from Governor Fred M. Warner on until 2 o'clock Wednesday morning, when he retired in the vain search of a few hours refreshing rest; for he had been working with all his might for several weeks. Thursday was the last session of the legislature; that day must tell the story.

"Just as his hopes had been low, so his joy was great when he heard the news in the morning that the house had reported the bill out and passed it, his work the night previous having made enough converts to enable Representative Trabbic to get through his motion to reconsider the action of Tuesday.

"It will be remembered that the movement for getting a monument began with considerable flourish early in the year and that, after a great deal of writing, pamphleting and signing of petitions, there was a sudden stop in all the proceedings. Much hard and earnest work had been done and many promises obtained from legislators, but politics had blocked everything. And everybody lost hope. Then those in charge of the movement turned in desperation to Fr. Crowley. When the committee was being selected, his name had been mentioned and he had been as much as told that he would be one of the members, but when the names were announced his name was missing. We can imagine his feelings when the committee came to him. The bill will reach Governor Warner in about a week, and on Wednesday he informed Fr. Crowley that he would sign it and then present it to Mrs. Custer with the pen with which he did so, Fr. Crowley to make the presentation."

• • •

The memorial association of 1907 grew out of a meeting of business men early that year at which a committee of Charles E. Greening, Fred A. Nims and Captain J. S. Harrington was named to ask the state for a $25,000 appropriation. The original plan was to purchase the old Bacon home, occupied also by the Custers, at Second and Monroe streets, which was still standing, and convert the site, now that of the post office, into a park for the monument. The city council and the Monroe Civic Improvement Society endorsed the plan. At a citizens' meeting on January 3 the committee was enlarged to include John M. Bulkley, Harry A. Conant, Burton Parker, James V. Barry, then state insurance commissioner, Judge C. B. Grant of Lansing, Senators Russell A. Alger and Julius C. Burrows, President James B. Angell of the University of Michigan and Congressman Charles E. Townsend.

Mayor George F. Heath had previously named representatives of the council and of the civic improvement society to serve on the committee. The ladies' organization was represented by Mrs. W. Van Miller, Mrs. J. J. Hubble and Miss Jenny

T. Sawyer. The council was represented by Mayor Heath, Frank G. Strong, Charles Hoyt and Dr. H. C. Orvis. In the final organization, Mr. Nims served as president of the committee, Mayor Heath as vice president, Mr. Greening as secretary and treasurer. Enlisted to assist in the drive for state funds, but not members of the committee, were State Senator Cline of Lenawee County and Representative F. H. Trabbic of Monroe County.

President Nims, in August, made the following report on the success of the undertaking: "Governor Warner's appointment of a Custer Monument Commission composed of the three men who were most intimate with the soldier both in war and society is the last happening in a long chain of efforts made by Michigan to pay permanent tribute to hero. It was an enormous body that fell into line and concentrated the weight of their influence at the capital city to obtain the appropriation for the monument. But the nucleus of the attempts originated here in Monroe. Last winter it was suggested that the city should begin proceedings toward asking the legislature for a sum to erect a monument in this city to General Custer. Mayor Heath chose a committee of three to unite with three from the council and three women of the civic improvement society, together forming a monument committee of ten including the Mayor.

• • •

"This little body immediately began to push the matter, to enlist the interest of people from other cities and to attract the attention of the state as well as of the city. Prominent men throughout Michigan, including our Congressman, judges of the supreme and courts, etc., were added to the first number. Then the Michigan Cavalry Brigade, which had begun a similar movement, joined forces with them. This brigade, over which Custer was placed as brigadier general, was peculiar inasmuch as it was the only one in the Union Army made up entirely of men from one state.

They numbered 4,800 soldiers, took a leading part in subduing the rebellion, and returned to Michigan in 1865 with few more than half of those who enlisted. (Mr. Nims himself served in the brigade as an aide to Custer.) With regard to the monument they had failed every time, but the comrades kept the subject alive among them and responded enthusiastically to the summons of our committee.

"Our committee did an overwhelming amount of correspondence and in the manner kept in touch with the brigade and were still continuing to solicit aid from wider circles. Our G.A.R. Post too sent out letters urging the monument bill to every Grand Army post in the state, and the vim with which the hundreds of stations took hold of the affair added 20 times the strength acquired when the brigade joined. Those who gave their time and talent to the Custer Memorial concert helped materially in supplying funds for the correspondence. When our representatives visited the legislature at Lansing in March they found that the request had met with much favor. Yet financially it was more than a pinch to donate $25,000 after the state had been to the appalling expense about its prisons, asylums, charitable institutions and educational matters. Our citizens argued that they were not asking for a monument for the dead but for the living and that the government could not afford to refuse to place the figure of Michigan's leading soldier before the eyes of our school boys, even though they were spending thousands on criminals, on the insane and the incompetent.

"Since the appointing of the commission to attend to the execution of the work, the council has shown its good will by giving a desirable site for the monument. The statue will be an equestrian one of General Custer as he looked when riding into battle. It is to be placed at the intersection of Washington and First streets on the spot where he played marbles when a boy, and but a few steps from the church in which he was married, when at the age of 27 he was already brigadier general in the Army of the Potomac. And if one looks deeply into the matter, one will find that Mrs. Custer's work and devotion to the object has had no small share in influencing the Custer monument bill, for the wife of the 'man who never surrendered' has herself in the 30 years since the war never surrendered her cause, to keep the memory of her husband alive in the minds of coming generations."

• • •

Thus came about the erection and dedication, in June, 1910, of the Custer monument, with Mrs. Custer herself present to cut the cord unveiling the statue and President Taft delivering the dedicatory address. As Mr. Nims wrote, Mrs. Custer was diligent in keeping her husband's memory alive. When the earlier Monroe monument association gave in to eastern sponsors and turned its money over to the New York Herald monument fund, a statue of the general was prepared for his grave at West Point. Mrs. Custer, on seeing it for the first time, disapproved, and it was removed from the grave. Many years later, when the Custer monument was moved from the courthouse square to Soldiers and Sailors Park, Mrs. Custer also disapproved and never thereafter visited her old home in Monroe.

June 23, 1951

- *75th Anniversary*
- *Museum Dedication*
- *7th Cavalry's Place*
- *Custer Battlefield*

MONDAY is the 75th anniversary of the Battle of the Little Big Horn. That engagement with the Sioux Indians, who were violating a military order by refusing to return to their reservation in western North Dakota, wiped out to a man five companies of the U. S. 7th Cavalry Regiment, commanded by General George Armstrong Custer. The only survivor from the onslaught of Chief Gall and Chief Crazy Horse on the banks of the Little Big Horn in southeastern Montana was Commanche, the mount of Captain Keough. Monroe lost, in that desperate Indian conflict on the plains, its greatest citizen, General Custer, his two brothers, Tom, a captain, and Boston, a civilian, the general's nephew, Armstrong Reed, also a civilian, and Lieutenant James Calhoun, who married Custer's favorite sister, Maggie.

It is a rather strange circumstance that Monroe's place in history was largely made by two Indian massacres. One was the slaughter of nearly 400 Kentuckians here in the War of 1812 by the lake Indians, egged on by British General Henry Proctor. The other was the annihilation of General Custer's command of 231 7th Cavalrymen and a dozen civilians on June 25, 1876.

Monday's anniversary furnishes another opportunity for the West, which regards Custer as the man who freed it from Indian domination, despite his ultimate defeat, to pay tribute to the general. At the Custer Battlefield National Monument near Hardin, Montana, Monday will be the occasion for the dedication of the new and splendid Custer Museum. A crowd of 25,000 Indians and whites, the former from the nearby Crow Reservation, is expected to watch the dedication ceremonies from 10 a.m. till noon. Significant of the

Army's veneration of George Armstrong Custer will be the appearance of Lieutenant General Albert C. Wedemeyer as orator of the day. General Wedemeyer, of course, has just completed his appearance before the Senate committees conducting the MacArthur hearing. Moreover, the sponsoring committee for the dedication has the promise of General George C. Marshall, just back from a Korean mission, to appear on the program if his schedule permits.

• • •

In conjunction with the dedication ceremonies, the state of Montana is holding a buffalo hunt for distinguished guests. The Crow Indians are conducting their annual tribal ceremonies and fair at the same time on their reservation, adjacent to the battlefield. Invited to participate in the dedication ceremonies are two Monroe men, Colonel Brice C. W. Custer, grandnephew of the general, now stationed at Fort Missoula, Montana, and Dr. L. A. Frost, past president of the Monroe County Historical Society and a Custer collector and scholar. Colonel Custer, incidentally, was the speaker at the Memorial Day observance at the battlefield. Among other distinguished guests for the dedication will be Colonel Wild Bill Harris, just back from Korea where he commanded the U. S. 7th Cavalry Regiment, now mechanized, in action. Colonel Custer, Colonel Harris and Dr. Frost will be house guests for the occasion of Colonel Edward S. Luce, superintendent of the battlefield monument.

Colonel Luce, who has spent several extended visits in Monroe in research on General Custer, is the man largely responsible for erection and establishment of the new Custer Museum at the battlefield. He won War Department and Congressional approval for the building, and has spent several years obtaining authorizations for transfer of authentic Custer material from the Smithsonian Insitution, West Point and other Army installations.

The museum building itself is scheduled for completion July 21. Colonel Luce expects it will take about a year to install the exhibits which he has collected, and hopes to have the formal opening a year from Monday on the 76th anniversary of the battle. When this occurs, visitors to the battlefield will find in the museum by far the most complete collection of Custer material in the world.

• • •

Monroe of course could not hope to compete with the West in observance of the battle anniversary. Custer and the legend of the 7th Regiment never made the impact on the East that they did on the West. Everywhere Custer and his regiment camped or fought in the plains states the spot is marked, and communities vie with one another in attracting tourists to historical sites connected with Custer's name. Six of the western states, formed out of the vast territory from which Custer drove or pacified the Indians, have named counties in his honor. The road along which the battlefield stands, now US-87, was named the Custer Memorial Highway all the way from Des Moines, Iowa, to Glacier National Park. Near the battlefield is the Custer National Forest. And in South Dakota, which Custer opened to settlement by his exploration of the Black Hills and discovery of gold, the largest state park in the country is named for him. A post office near the battlefield is named Garryowen for the 7th's famed battlesong.

However, Monroe is going to pay tribute to Custer Monday on the battle anniversary. The Monroe County Historical Society is sponsoring a patriotic ceremony at the Custer Monument in Soldiers and Sailors Park. The community that Custer always regarded as his home, though it was not this birthplace, thus shares in the reflected glory of the anniversary.

Westerners never have neglected an opportunity to exploit the Custer legend. Twenty-five years ago, on June 25, 1926, the 50th anniversary of the battle was celebrated for three days at Hardin. Indians from the reservations in all the nearby states were invited to Hardin, and with U. S. Cavalry troops reenacted the famous Last Stand. Mrs. Custer, then living in New York, was invited to attend, but thought best not to revive old memories by doing so. Instead she listened dry-eyed and silent to a radio broadcast of the battle.

• • •

Colonel Luce has written a graphic account of the battle and the events leading up to it, of the part played by Custer and the 7th in the opening of the West, and of the battlefield monument itself in the historical handbook published by the National Park Service. In one paragraph he sums up the reasons why Custer is so much more revered in the West than in the East:

"The 7th Cavalry's record under General Custer well illustrates the important part played by the United States Army in the advance of frontier settlements. Stationed at remote army posts and isolated cantonments, they were called on to guard emigrants and freighters, mail stages and telegraph lines. Sometimes they undertook exploring expeditions into little-known regions, and sometimes they protected scientific expeditions into new territory. They shielded surveyors laying out the route for railroads, and the construction crews who built the roads. Sometimes they evicted white trespassers from Indian reservations, and some they risked their lives in campaigns against the Indians."

In 1879, three years after the battle, the Federal Government made the battlefield a national monument – the Arlington of the West. This is Colonel Luce's description of battlefield at present: "The principal feature of Custer Battlefield National Monument is the battlefield, marked by the memorial which stands over the grave of most of the slain victims of the battle. This memorial is about one-half mile beyond the main entrance to the area. From this fenced, granite shaft is obtained an excellent view of the field over which occurred the final stages of Custer's last battle. White markers, scattered over the hillsides, show as nearly as possible where the dead were found (three days) after their struggle was over.

• • •

Just below the memorial is a small group of markers indicating the sites where General Custer and those nearest him in battle were found. Two brothers of the general, Captain Thomas Ward Custer and Boston Custer, with their nephew, Autie Reed, were also found in this group. A road from the memorial leads along the ridge from which can be seen the rough terrain over which the men fought. Groups of markers to the right on the slope toward the river tell the story of how Companies C and E fought to their death. A number of bodies were found in deep ravines near the river. Some markers cannot be seen, for they are concealed by the rolling contour of the slopes. Beyond these markers and across the river is the location of the Indian encampment at the time of the battle.

"About one-half mile from the memorial on a loop road to the left is an interpretive sign at the position where Company L made its last stand. Lieutenant Calhoun, a brother-in-law of General Custer, was in command of this company. According to those who buried the soldiers on June 28, 1876, the bodies of these men showed the most clearly drawn skirmish line on the battlefield.

"Just beyond the loop road at Calhoun Hill, the road turning to the right leads to the Reno-Benteen battlefield entrenchments, four miles to the southeast. This road drops down very near to the Little Big Horn River. It was at this point, which was about the center of the Indian encampment, that the Sioux Chief Gall crossed to make his first attack on Custer's battalion. They met Custer about three-fourths of a mile northeast of that ford. In about two miles, the road is cut through the high point from which Captain Weir and his company viewed Custer's battlefield on the afternoon of June 25. It is the farthest point any of Reno's or Benteen's men reached before being forced back. A mile and a half farther is the 7th Cavalry Memorial on the Reno-Benteen battlefield. This location affords a fine view of the valley where Major Reno's battalion fought and of their retreat route up the rugged bluffs."

July 26, 1952

- *Custer Museum*
- *Dedication Ceremony*
- *Mementoes of the 7th*
- *Libby's Collection*

ON the 76th anniversary of the Battle of the Little Big Horn, June 25, a new federal museum was dedicated with appropriate ceremonies at the site of the battle in Montana. M. H. Morrison of Flat Rock, who attended the dedication, has furnished The Observer with this account of the program taken from the Denver Post: "Seventy-six years after Custer and his men made their final stand against the Indians, a new museum will be dedicated to the growing interest in this historic spot. The Battle of the Little Big Horn, officials said, each year is seizing the imaginations of more and more Americans in their western tours. The new museum will be a major attraction to visitors.

"General Jonathan 'Skinny' Wainwright, hero of Bataan, will place a wreath on the monument on Custer Hill, where lie the bodies of about 220 cavalrymen who died with their commander. The new museum was built by the National Park Service, which operates Custer Battlefield National Monument. Construction of the museum is the out-growth of a long campaign on the part of Montanans for a place to house relics of the historic battle. They give much of the credit to Captain and Mrs. Edward S. Luce. Luce is superintendent of the battlefield and a retired officer of the 7th Cavalry, the military group that left its dead on the field in 1876.

"For more than a decade, the Luces have worked on planning the museum and have collected, authenticated and cataloged hundreds of relics and documents relating to the battle. Mr. Luce has conducted lectures each week for visitors. In addition to care of the battlefield, Luce also superintends the national military cemetery. Remains of soldiers from every American war since the Indian wars lie here. The museum, which cost $100,000, puts emphasis on telling the story of the battle in sequence form. An exact scale diorama depicts the formation of Custer's troops. The story is told progressively from there until the last man is dead.

● ● ●

"While Lieutenant Colonel George A. Custer and his men were engaging the Indians on the hill overlooking the Little Big Horn River, Major Marcus Reno and Captain Frederick W. Benteen were commanding battalions in the same area. The movement of these groups until their rescue by General Terry also is shown in the dioramas. The last white soldier in the engagement, Sergeant Charles Windolph of Lead, South Dakota, who served with Benteen, died about three years ago. Officials have sent invitations to the Standing Rock, Pine Ridge and Rosebud Sioux Indian Reservations in South Dakota to attend the dedication. Wainwright will give the museum a Winchester rifle found on the battlefield that was given to him by a survivor many years ago."

Captain Luce has spent some time at Monroe continuing his research on Custer. From Dr. L. A. Frost, The Observer borrowed another newspaper account of the museum. Dr. Frost attended the ceremony a year ago at the laying of the cornerstone for the museum, but was unable to be at the dediction. This account, from the Billings, Montana, Gazette, reads in part:

"The Custer memorial first was erected in March and April of 1879 by a detachment of the 11th U. S. Infantry stationed at old Fort Custer and under the command of Captain G. K. Sanderson. The monument commemorates the events of one of the most heatedly-discussed afternoons in American history – the afternoon when Lieutenant Colonel Custer, 7th, Cavalry, and 250 of his command fell before the onslaught of the Sioux and Cheyenne. Another page will be added to the Custer legend when the recently completed Custer Memorial Museum will be opened to the public. Colonel W. A. 'Wild Bill' Harris, liberator of Seoul, Korea and commander of the 7th during some of the toughest engagements in Korea, will talk on the present U. S. 7th Cavalry and the esprit d'corps that has made it the most famous regiment in the Army.

• • •

"Colonel Brice C. W. Custer, grandnephew of the general, will give a resume of the history of the Custer family, Ronald F. Lee, assistant director of the National Park Service, will give the welcome, and Governor John W. Bonner of Montana will respond. District Judge Ben Harwood of Billings will give the dedication address, followed by remarks about the museum by Captain Luce. The climax will be General Wainwright's presentation of the Winchester found on the battlefield, which has been in the Wainwright family since 1887. In that year General Wainwright's father, Lieutenant Robert P. P. Wainwright, was stationed at Fort Custer. He engaged in a skirmish with the Ghost Shirts, a cult of Crows, shot one of the Indians who dropped the rifle, and it was retrieved by a trumpeteer in the troop. Two Whistles, the wounded Crow, had been a scout with General Gibbon, and two days after the battle had been on burial duty at the battlefield, when he picked up the rifle, believed to have been used by a Sioux or Cheyenne.

"Colonel Custer will cut the red, white and blue ribbon sealing the museum door, thus opening it officially to the public. The museum, which also houses the administrative offices, is of modern design, built of cinder block. It is located midway between the cemetery buildings, erected in 1894, and Custer Hill. The building is angled in such a way that the view from the terrace stretches south to Garryowen, Montana, the vicinity in which Reno first engaged the Indians, the valley through which Reno retreated, the Indian encampment, Weir Point, Custer Ridge and Custer Hill.

"Entering the museum room proper, the visitor's attention is directed to a display of photographs of the officers who gave their lives during the two days of June 25 and 26, with the point of interest being an original copy of the Bismarck Tribune, dated July 6, 1876, which carried part of the famous telegraph story Colonel Lounsbury, Tribune editor, sent to the New York Herald. Next is a large diorama entitled Custer's Last Stand, the background centered with a figure of Custer in authentic costume. Every man and horse is accurate to the minutest detail. The figure of Custer, with his Webley English revolvers ablaze, is dressed in gray hat, red neck piece, blue jacket and frontier breeches. At his feet lies a three-inch-long carbine with a realistic jammed shot.

• • •

"Moving to the right, the visitor finds a chronological display of the events that culminated in the Custer annihilation. First is the discovery of gold in the Black Hills of South Dakota. Next is a poster showing how the Army moved in to bring the Indians into the Sioux reservation. An orientation map of Custer on the march is flanked by a copy of Terry's orders to Custer. Cavalry arms and equipment are displayed, and there is a graphic painting of the Indian encampment and photographs of the Sioux and Cheyenne chiefs in the battle, including Sitting Bull.

A case features Indian weapons of the time, including war clubs, Sharps rifles and steel-tipped arrows. How Custer divided his forces is shown on a poster, with arrows pointing out the directions they took and the proportionment of troops among Reno, Custer, Benteen and McDougall, the latter guarding the pack-train. 'What happened to Custer' is depicted, with authentic weapons from the battle and a painting. A second diorama tells the story of Reno's retreat. Diaries of cavalrymen found on the battlefield are displayed.

"Photos from the collection of Elizabeth Bacon Custer illustrate typical contemporary cavalry tactics. The museum is arranged in such a way that the display in the west end deals with the story of the actual battle, while the east end is given over to the major participants. Here are displays of Indian articles, including pieces of clothing removed from the bodies of the soldiers and retrieved from the Indians at the Battle of Slim Buttes, Dakota territory, in September, 1876.

• • •

"The south wall is a display of the life of Custer beginning with his West Point career. All materials here are from the Elizabeth Bacon Custer collection. In one case are his West Point cadet jacket, his presidential appointment, his diploma and commission as a second lieutenant. Here is an original composition entitled 'Red Man' which Custer wrote in his ethics course at the academy. Custer in the Civil War is the title of the next case and is followed by one telling of Custer on the plains. His famous white buckskin jacket and breeches, which were given to the Big Horn county public library by Mrs. Custer, are displayed. It is believed that five guidons were carried into combat and the museum has one of these last flags to follow Custer into battle. It is on loan from the Detroit Art Institute.

The final display is the graphic history of the gallant 7th Cavalry from its formation at Fort Riley, Kansas, in 1866 to its present-day activities in Korea and Japan. The focus is a concentric circle, forming a spiral history wheel and building from the regiment insignia – a horseshoe carrying seven nails and centered with an arm and sabre. The orientation room on the terrace gives a complete view of the valley, the ridge and the hill. Here is a relief map showing the topography of the entire battlefield, and enabling the visitor to take an armchair tour of the terrain."

Many thousands of visitors, enthralled by the Custer legend, will throng the new museum out in Montana this year and in the years to come. But right here in Monroe we have an exhibit of Custer material that in many ways is more interesting and more complete than that at the battlefield. Yet for lack of finances, and of local appreciation of the nationwide appeal of the Custer legend, the museum and its Custer display remain closed during the summer season. The same tourists who will drive all the way to Montana would throng the local museum if proper provisions could be made to keep it open and publicize it.

January 3, 1953

- *Custer Still News*
- *The Court-Martial*
- *Was It Custer's Body?*
- *Custer Hunting Rifle*

LOOKING for copy for a new gun collectors' publication, "Great Guns," Bill Palmer, son of Dearborn's Andy Palmer, visited the Monroe County Historical Museum. Bill got plenty; the December issue of his paper has half a dozen stories about Monroe's famed Indian fighter and Civil War hero, General George A. Custer. The story is told of how Adolphus Busch, founder of Anheuser-Busch, had the painting of Custer's Last Fight reproduced as an advertisement for the brewery. That lurid and hardly accurate chromo since has been distributed in more than a million copies, testifying to popular interest in Custer lore.

Dr. Lawrence A. Frost, past president of the Monroe County Historical Society, contributed a touch of authentic history in his account of the court-martial at which General Custer was deprived of pay and rank for a year for allegedly deserting his troops. Custer and his wife, Libby Bacon Custer, returned to Monroe, whence he was summoned to engage in his last battle. Dr. Frost's story of the court-martial follows:

"The inside story of the Custer court-martial has never been told in its entirety. Few folks know that General Custer was sentenced at Fort Leavenworth, Kansas, back in 1867, to forfeit his rank and pay for one year. The way this all came about is most interesting. It dates back to the Indian uprisings along the routes of the railroads and highways that crossed Kansas, early in the spring of that year.

● ● ●

In 1866 Indian agents had been giving out large numbers of

arms and ammunitions to the Sioux and Cheyennes so that they might obtain game more easily, this to the objection of the military. All of the Indians were observed to have revolvers, a large majority having two and many having three. An expedition against the warring Indians was commenced by General Winfield S. Hancock, a man of little Indian experience but with a fine Civil War background. General Hancock had learned that the Oglalla and Brule Sioux had come down from the north to arrange general hostilities with the aid of the Cheyenne and the Dog Soldiers 'when the grass begins to grow.'

"Hancock's move was to order out the newly organized Seventh Cavalry under General George Armstrong Custer and, in addition, the 37th Infantry with light battery B and the Fourth Artillery. He proceeded to the region of Forts Zarah, Larned and Dodge on the Arkansas River, as well as Forts Hays and Harker on the Smoky Hill River. It was Hancock's express desire to show the Indians that he was prepared for war, although the restoration of peace and the arrest of the miscreants was his primary purpose in asking them to sit in council with him.

"On April 13, 1867, Hancock approached a semi-deserted village of over 300 Sioux and Cheyenne lodges camped on the Pawnee Fork and on April 19, after the escaping Indians failed to return, burned the village. General Custer had been ordered after the escaping Indians, which order he complied with by following their main trail. After a long forced march he came close enough to their rear to observe moisture in the pony tracks. Taking alarm at the nearness of their pursuers, the Indians split up into small parties, taking to dry creek beds and hard ground in order to cover up the trail.

• • •

"The trails were soon lost and Custer found it necessary to turn toward Fort Hays. Lookout Station was found burned to the ground with the bodies of three murdered men laying nearby, obviously the work of the Indians. Arriving at Fort Hays, he found but one day's supply of grain although two months prior, General Hancock had ordered an eight to ten day's supply of forage to be placed there for the expedition. As a result, Custer was unable to pursue the Indians whose horses were growing weak from lack of forage. Of the events that followed, Custer's court-martial was the climax. On September 16, 1867, Custer appeared before a general court-martial at Fort Leavenworth on charges of:

"1 – Absence from his command without leave; 2 – Failure to take proper measures to repulse the Indians or recover the bodies of his dead; 3 – Giving orders to shoot down a group of deserters and to bring in none alive; 4 – Refusing to permit the wounded deserters to receive proper medical attention; 5 – Using army ambulances and mules as a conveyance on private business.

"The trial occupied the better part of September and October after which Custer retired to the Fort Leavenworth apartments of General Sheridan which had been offered him as long as he desired. In the spring of 1868 Custer returned to Monroe to enjoy the companionship of old friends in boating, fishing and hunting. The Indian campaign in the summer of 1868 did not go along too well for the army and in a telegram dated September 24, 1868, at Fort Hays, General Sheridan wired: 'Generals Sherman, Sully and myself, and nearly all the officers of your regiment, have asked for you, and I hope the application will be successful. Can you come at once?' "

• • •

Another Custer authority, E. A. Brininstool of the Los Angeles Times, also contributes an article on Custer. "There is speculation nowadays, 76 years after the Battle of the Little Big Horn, as to whether the remains supposed to be those of the noted cavalry leader are really his which were exhumed and reburied at West Point," Brininstool writes. "It is a question which probably never was, or will be, satisfactorily determined. All the published reports state that after General Gibbons' troops, accompanied by detachments from Reno's command, went over the Custer battlefield on Tuesday, June 27, two days after the battle, they 'buried the dead.'

"All told, there were 260 officers and men killed in Custer's and Reno's commands, those on the Custer field numbering approximately 220 to 225. There were very few shovels or picks in the relief column and there had not been any such tools taken along with Custer's command when it left Fort Lincoln, never for a moment thinking they would have any use for them.

"Sergeant M. C. Caddle of Troop I, under Captain Myles Keogh, was one of the men detailed from the troop to remain at the Powder River camp in charge of the Seventh Cavalry's property. Every other trooper of Keogh's command was killed. In June, 1877, Caddle, owing to his acquaintance with the officers and men of his regiment, and especially those of Keogh's troop, was detailed to accompany the burial party under Colonel Michael Sheridan, a brother of General Phil Sheridan. Another officer who assisted was Colonel H. W. Wheeler, who lived with my family following his retirement and from whom I have many times listened to his account.

• • •

"Sergeant Caddle states that when they arrived on the field they found all the skeletons lying on top of the ground, the bodies apparently having been dug up and mutilated by wolves and coyotes. It would therefore appear that no serious attempt was made to inter the bodies of the dead on June 27, 1876. The ground was as hard as flint, and as there were not over two or three spades it would have been impossible to properly inter the bodies.

"Colonel Sheridan remained on the field ten days, during which the bones were placed in coffins. Each body when buried the year before had been marked with a stake at its head, with a number to correspond with the name. Among those was one supposed to be that of General Custer. The remains of a blouse were found, and in the pocket was a name, but it was not the name of General Custer. It was a most disconcerting discovery to find that not even the remains of the noted cavalry leader could be satisfactorily identified, but Sergeant Caddle states that 'we found another body and placed it in a coffin intended for the remains of General Custer. I think we got the right body the second time.'

"It is popularly supposed that the distribution of the headstones about the fenced monument at the battlefield represents the exact spot where certain of the officers fell in the fight, but there is nothing to substantiate this theory."

• • •

The scattering of the bones from the shallow graves, as described by Mr. Brininstool, bears a marked resemblance to the fate that befell the Kentuckians killed in the battle and massacre of the River Raisin 63 years before the Custer massacre. Custer's bones, or those of a comrade, were recovered a year later and interred at West Point, while those of the Kentuckians were moved about Monroe several times and taken to Detroit before finally being interred at Lexington.

• • •

Bill Palmer's visit to the museum also served to authenticate a gun in the Custer collection as one he had used in hunting. The rifle came to the society from the Custer family, and was shipped to Monroe along with Custer's horse, Dandy, a trunk and other possessions by the army. Palmer found the gun was not a GI Springfield, but had a shortened forearm stock and special double set trigger and trigger guard. A photo in the museum shows General Custer holding the gun and dressed in buckskin hunting costume. Palmer also identified the gun in a series of pictures taken when Custer escorted Grand Duke Alexis of Russia on a Buffalo hunt on the western plains.

Custeriana Monograph Series includes the following:

1. *The Life of General Custer*
    By Milton Ronsheim

2. *The Kid*
    by Elizabeth B. Custer

3. *Historical Sketches of General Custer*
    by James H. Kidd

4. *Custer's Last Battle*
    by Richard A. Roberts

5. *Frazier Hunt's Story of General Custer*

6. *Yellowhair*
    by Charles G. Tayor and Jason Kane

7. *The Glory March*
    by Kenneth M. Hammer

8. *Last Statement to Custer*
    by John S. Manion

9. *Witnesses at the Battle of the Little Big Horn*
    by Earle R. Forrest

10. *General Custer's Photographers*
    by Dr. Lawrence A. Frost

11. *Custer Observed: General Custer Through the Eyes of Monroe Evening News' Karl Zeisler*

*Number Eleven
of the Monroe County Library System's
Custeriana Monograph Series*

This is number

004

*of a limited edition
of three hundred.*

The acid free paper on which this limited edition book is printed has an effective life of at least 300 years.